REPUTATION MATRIX

MATRIX

Five Strategies to Increase your Visibility,
Credibility, and Positive Word of Mouth
in the Community and Online

MARJORIE YOUNG

Reputation Matrix
Five Strategies to Increase your Visibility, Credibility, and
Positive Word of Mouth in the Community and Online
All Rights Reserved.
Copyright © 2020 Marjorie Young
v3.0

Carriage Trade Publishing II, Inc.

ISBN: 978-0-578-23251-5

Library of Congress Control Number: 2020908973

Cover design by Longwater & Company. Cover Photo © 2020 Marjorie Young. All rights reserved.

PRINTED IN THE UNITED STATES OF AMERICA

Dedication

To my entrepreneurial parents, Carol and Dave Watson, who owned and operated a true mom-and-pop business publishing community magazines in Washington, DC. They taught me the importance not only of owning my own company, but also of owning my own life. And to my daughter, Carol Christine Young, PhD, who is my constant cheerleader.

Reviews

Melissa Gratias, PhD, Productivity Coach, Speaker, and Writer

"*Reputation Matrix* turns small business marketing on its head. I am a small business owner and thought that word of mouth was outside of my control. Marjorie Young's book has empowered me to make word of mouth an active marketing practice that I cultivate rather than something I just cross my fingers and hope to receive. This is a game changer!"

Tommy Barton, Former Editorial Page Editor of *Savannah Morning News* and President of I Am Not Old News

"Word-of-mouth publicity is the secret sauce of marketing. All businesses want it, but relatively few have an idea or a plan of how to make it happen. Veteran Savannah PR guru Marjorie Young unveils the recipe and ingredients in her new book, *Reputation Matrix.* As the operator of a new company that specializes in travel and food blogging, I found what is in essence a 'cookbook' breakdown of PR to be invaluable, easy to read, and packed with useful information that I'm sure to use as I build my own brand. Marjorie's *Reputation Matrix* should be on the shelf of any businessperson who cares about his or her reputation and influence."

Roy Austin, Author of *The Alligator Business Solution: Small Business Competitive Advantage*

"I am a firm believer in systematizing business functions to improve productivity, efficiency, on-boarding of new employees, etc. In *Reputation Matrix,* Marjorie Young shows how to systematize the public relations function to maximize impact, gain and keep customers, and grow your business. If you are serious about growing your business you must read this book. Marjorie breaks PR down into bite-sized, easily digestive points that you can quickly implement. Her matrix can be adapted to systematize other business functions, making the book an extremely valuable addition to your knowledge. I highly recommend *Reputation Matrix.*"

Terrass "Razz" Misher, Pod On The Go

"A huge turning point in my life and business was moving to Savannah and meeting Marjorie. I've interviewed hundreds of small business owners, read countless business books, and listened to literally thousands of hours of business podcasts and nothing compares to the principles Marjorie shares in this book. *Reputation Matrix* is so powerful that it's almost guaranteed to grow your business, make an impact in your community, and lead you on a path toward fulfillment in business and in life.

Through Marjorie's friendship and mentorship, I not only learned a proven method for business growth with *Reputation Matrix*, but (more importantly), I was given hope that my start-up niche business idea could actually make a difference in my community. And I'm positive reading this book will do the same for you."

Suzana Barton, President of Happy Great Day

"Building my new company from the ground up felt like climbing a mountain. I couldn't see the top! I was gripped with fear of the unknown, which included everything from material costs and vendor expenses to taxes and trademark fees. This book is the Ninja Business Skills Roadmap that put me on track. Now I've got an Excel spreadsheet, which identifies every step I'm taking on my running start, and an annual marketing plan. *Reputation Matrix* has helped me replace self-doubt with confidence and joy."

Nipuna Ambanpola, Cofounder and Executive Director, IVolunteer International

"As a start-up nonprofit organization, IVolunteer International will utilize the *Reputation Matrix* guidebook to establish trust within the local communities we impact across the globe. *Reputation Matrix* has not only enabled us to realize the value of our brand, but has also empowered us to strategize our public relations efforts with reinforced agility. *Reputation Matrix* is a living guide that we will revisit every year as we work to build our brand around the positive impact we are having on the world."

Bonnie Rachael, CEO of Faith Equestrian Therapeutic Center Inc.

"I'm so excited about this book! It is encouraging, honest, and insightful. It is a reminder to me that I need to stay on track of what Marjorie, a mentor of mine, has already taught me. I get so busy with the daily grind I let the PR slide sometimes, and I so appreciate the shot in the arm this little book provides; I'm renewed and encouraged in my PR spirit! I can use this to re-mind myself to get out there, and not a minute too soon. This is a must-read for the nonprofit world. Most nonprofits have no room in their budgets for advertising, nor do they know where to start in raising awareness for their good works. Thank you, Marjorie, for sharing your wisdom and experience so others can be successful entrepreneurs too!"

Table of Contents

Preface

If you run a small business and would like to be better known in your community and online, this guidebook is for you.

It begins with knowing that the majority of new business comes from positive word of mouth.

What's easy to forget—and may be surprising—is that mega-positive word of mouth comes from a planned strategy.

In the following pages, I will share with you the top five strategies I have used with clients during my twenty-five years as a publicist. The same strategies also helped turn my father's business around. They help raise a positive buzz, build trust, and drive business growth in order to establish a powerful brand reputation in the community and online.

The "Reputation Matrix," as I have coined it, is a reputation management method used to help build your yearly PR plan and leverage your good business news to create ultrapositive word of mouth.

This proprietary strategy focuses on using my top five "credibility markers" to enhance the reputation of small business owners.

The time has come to take control of your brand!

Marjorie Young
President of Carriage Trade Public Relations® Inc.
Savannah, Georgia
January 2020

PART I:

Let's Give Them Something to Talk About

CHAPTER 1

Why Does Word of Mouth Matter?

Entrepreneur magazine defines *word of mouth* as "an unpaid form of promotion in which satisfied customers tell other people how much they like a business, product, or service."

The Merriam-Webster Dictionary defines *buzz* as "speculative or excited talk or attention relating especially to a new or forthcoming product."

Word-of-mouth marketing has been around for centuries. According to Nielsen, a global measurement and data analytics company, 92 percent of new business comes from word of mouth. That means that businesses rely on referrals more than any other type of marketing.

People communicate constantly. We talk about everything. Check out all the TV talk shows, radio shows, newspaper columns, and social media chats. It is part of being human. As a business, you have to find a way into the conversation.

If word of mouth is so powerful, why aren't more business owners implementing word-of-mouth campaigns to help market their company? My guess is that they do not realize there is an actual strategy to help build their reputations by boosting their positive buzz in the community and online.

I am a publicist who has worked with small and large business owners and nonprofit organizations for twenty-five years. People come to my firm for many reasons; these are the most common:

- They need better visibility in the community and online for better sales.
- They want to increase the value of their business in preparation for a sale.
- They have tried other types of marketing to little or no avail.
- They are combating negative publicity and negative word of mouth.
- They are launching a new company.
- They are launching a capital campaign or fundraiser.
- They are preparing their company to go public.
- They are trying to avoid bankruptcy.

The last reason is a little extreme, but this is where I learned firsthand the power of public relations in helping to boost positive word of mouth, and in turn increased sales.

Public relations (PR) is about marketing your business. As I will explain in chapter 3, it is not "marketing" in the sense of sales. It is about building your reputation in the community and online.

Your reputation is built slowly over time through constant demonstrations of the reliability and trustworthiness of your organization.

Your reputation is built by doing well in business and by doing good things for the community.

Your reputation is built by having people say positive things about you and your business. Over time you establish real trust.

John D. Rockefeller once said, "Next to doing the right thing, the most important thing is to let people know you are doing the right thing." Your business will soar by letting the media know about your good news.

The public relations (PR) strategies that I am going to share with you in this guidebook helped my father's company avoid bankruptcy during a recession.

They have also helped hundreds of my clients over the past twenty-five years.

Each of them plays a role in creating your own positive buzz by using a set of guidelines I call the Reputation Matrix. The

Reputation Matrix is, at its core, a personalized plan that will lead to positive word of mouth for your business.

The book you are now holding will walk you through five strategies for turning your community involvement into big-time word of mouth by capitalizing on traditional media outlets and helping you announce your good news consistently throughout the year.

This book will show you how we do it in the PR world.

CHAPTER 2

My Story
Lessons Learned from Our
Family Business in Crisis

In 1990 I was standing in the kitchen of our off-base housing in Nuremberg, West Germany, stirring a pot of spaghetti, when the phone rang.

It was my father calling from Alexandria, Virginia, where our family business was located. Almost as soon as I said hello, he got to the point: "I need to borrow ten thousand dollars for the print shop. We are having terrible cash flow at the office. This recession is horrible."

This came the day after my husband told me he was going to be deployed to the Gulf War.

I decided to fly back to the USA to help.

It took about two weeks to pack suitcases, buy airline tickets for my two-year-old daughter and me, and arrange for our cats, Puzza and Yankee, to fly back.

When my father picked us up at the Washington National Airport, we got my daughter into her car seat, and somehow found room for the two cat cages and our luggage.

The car was quiet as he turned onto the beltway and headed east, rather than toward what had been our family home. He had sold it to support the business.

During the drive I learned that we owed thousands of dollars to vendors, the Internal Revenue Service was demanding back payroll taxes, the state of Virginia was going to audit us for back sales taxes, and we had lost health insurance coverage due to nonpayment.

All of this came four years after my mother died of lung cancer at the age of fifty-four.

"The hell continues," I thought.

In the first week after my return, I unpacked and enrolled my daughter at a preschool close to the business. When I finally got to the newly relocated and less expensive industrial park office, I was greeted by the secretary, a full-time printer, and my two brothers. I was also greeted with a stack of mail that turned out to be late notices, ninety days past due, lien letters, and attempts to collect.

My heart sank.

I had no idea how we could get out of this hole but began by trying to get a bank loan. A courteous man in a brown suit listened as I tried to convince him to help us, but we now had zero collateral.

"No," he said politely.

However, he did offer me a free ticket to a business expo the bank was sponsoring a few blocks from the White House. The event was a huge eye-opener. Not only did I meet dozens of new prospects, I also realized the power of public speaking.

Each business owner who got onstage to share educational tips and advice was surrounded immediately by audience members who wanted more information about their products or services.

Afterward I set up an appointment with my father and a bankruptcy attorney. He reviewed our financial situation and agreed that our only option was to declare bankruptcy.

"However," he said, "you will still owe back payroll taxes, which are in the thousands and thousands of dollars."

"Well," my father said after a minute of silence, "there is only one thing to do. Somehow we need to get sales up."

After dinner, I got my daughter, Carol, to bed and drove back to the print shop. Inside, I stood in silence with the overwhelming smell of press cleaners and ink around me, listening to make sure I was alone.

Then I sat down in front of a pile of notices, bills, and threatening letters before I picked up the largest pile and carried it to an open space on the floor. I randomly examined dozens of invoices with a consistent theme: due immediately, action will be taken, overdue, $50,000 owed, pressing charges, late notice, lien, and suing!

I didn't know what to do. My father had already sold his house and his car, couldn't afford health insurance, and had just been diagnosed with prostate cancer.

I asked God for guidance and to please send me a sign.

When I looked up, I realized we didn't even have a sign in the new office window to let passersby know who we were. It felt like He was speaking loud and clear, "You need to market this company!"

I left the pile of papers and turned to a computer at the abandoned desk of an employee we had been forced to lay off the previous week.

I opened the design program and picked out the font Helvetica. I typed in 300-point size, but that only filled half the page. I tried again at 400, then 500, and finally 600. That filled the entire sheet of paper with the letter C.

After it was printed, I found a pair of scissors and carefully cut the letter out of the crisp white paper. By 1:00 a.m. I had printed and cut out each letter I would need to spell the company name. I found some clear tape and began sticking the letters along the top of our huge plate glass window. By the time the final letter was in place, it was 1:30 a.m.

The sign was complete.

On my way out the door, I noticed a trade publication titled *How to Market Your Print Shop* and took it with me.

As I sat in my car, I smiled at the new sign—Carriage Trade Printing—spanning our entire front window.

"We *can do this*!" I thought.

During the following evenings, after my daughter went to sleep, I would pull out the printing trade magazines that were mailed to us monthly and take notes on marketing ideas, cash flow solutions, and processes. It didn't take long to fill my one-hundred-page spiral notebook with ideas on how to beat this recession.

Many industry-specific articles were about the power of setting goals: "If you don't know where you are going, how will you know if you ever arrive?" Set attainable goals; they will keep you on track. That lesson has always stayed with me.

My father and I had long conversations about where our greatest profit margins were and what type of printing we could best accomplish with our equipment. Would we be printers for the medical field? Would we be printers for the schools? For associations? Once we decided on our market, I knew we could go after them aggressively.

Association printing kept coming back into our conversations. We already had a list of associations that were happy with our business. I asked my father to call some of them and ask what they liked most about doing business with us. "Marketing research" is what the trade publications dubbed this practice.

My father did call and found that they loved our quick response time, the fact we were neighbors and family owned, our free delivery and free storage, the beautiful work that my brother produced on the presses, and that the company had been around for a long time.

Our accountant wanted to charge us a lot of money to talk about the profitability of concentrating on one target market. So my next call was to SCORE, an organization that offers free business mentoring to this day. We looked at the numbers and decided to focus on associations. This type of printing involved long runs of letterheads and envelopes, which meant better profits for us and less time changing the plates and ink on the press.

We christened our new tagline: "Printers for Associations." It was memorable and easy to repeat when networking, and it also let our target market know we were experts in their field of printing. This was to be what I now call our "repeatable tagline."

Next we had to figure out which came first, marketing efforts or fending off creditors. For me, that meant spending the first part of the day working on cash flow, and the second part of the day working on marketing.

Over the next few evenings, I stacked up every invoice and created a basic spreadsheet. Unfortunately, this was before Excel. In the left-hand column, I listed the vendors to whom we owed money. In the next column, I wrote the amount due to each of the vendors. At the bottom of the vendor column, I added it all together. I stared at the six-digit number for a long time, hoping for an answer on how to pay it off.

When I divided the monster number by twelve months, the totals looked more manageable.

Once I knew what our actual costs were each month, it was easier to set a goal for how much we had to sell.

I decided to use the same spreadsheet format to line up marketing objectives for each month, which turned out to be a prototype for my Reputation Matrix. We had no budget for advertising, so we had to figure out how to make ourselves known without it.

Looking back, I realize most of what we did was create positive word of mouth in the community by getting an article in the newspaper, presenting talks, and doing basic networking. The spreadsheet helped me condense all my marketing "action items" onto one page, which made it easy for me to keep track of what I needed to do each month.

Both of my spreadsheets were drawn with a black pen and a ruler. Superstitiously, I didn't dare use a red pen, which represented being in debt. To this day, I don't like the color red.

My initial plan looked something like this:

I first figured out where to make sales calls and then called each of them to introduce myself and, hopefully, make an appointment.

My next action item was to create a series of postcards and send them to the potential clients I had called.

Next, I wrote a media release about the company's thirtieth year in business.

The following month, I planned to make more sales calls.

Then, using the database I had built of my calls, we launched a monthly educational newsletter.

I didn't have any of my textbooks from the University of Maryland with me on how to write media releases, but I did remember they needed to be one page, short and to the point, with no hint of endorsements. Just the facts.

I looked up the phone number of the local newspaper and called the business reporter. I told her that our family-owned business was about to turn thirty years old, and we would welcome a visit from her to talk about what it takes to run a business. After my pitch, I sent her the media release. Three days later, the woman called to say a reporter would stop by the next morning at 11:00 a.m.

The marketing plan was working.

I reminded my family to not mention anything negative to the reporter or to anybody who walked into our business. People love to ask, "How is your business?" It was always tempting to say that we were turning it around, but the trade publications advised against that because "nobody wants to do work with a failing business."

Instead they suggested staying positive and saying with a smile, "All is good. Thank you for asking."

The reporter spent about an hour asking questions and taking pictures before she requested the names of some of our clients and their contact information. I happily gave her our top two. I also called the customers to give them a heads-up that a reporter wanted to speak with them about our business. They were happy to help.

We got a flattering article on the front page of the business section, with a picture of my brother, my father, and me at work in the shop. It also included some powerful quotes about staying in business for thirty years.

It was, in essence, a third-party endorsement about how great our family-owned business was. My brother was able to create a smaller version of the article, and we printed it on 8½-inch by 11-inch paper to hand out at sales meetings. We also hung a copy on the wall so customers could see it when they stepped into our office.

That was when the hypothetical power of publicity and positive word of mouth became real to me. When clients saw this article, it reinforced their confidence in doing business with us.

Meanwhile, the IRS was demanding a back payroll payment. Finally, I invited an IRS agent, Mr. E. Washington, to the office. I explained to him that my mother had died just four years prior and that the recession was really hurting us. I assured him that despite the circumstances, we had a plan to repay the IRS and others to whom we owed money.

Earlier he had sent a letter proposing we pay back $5,000 a month, but before he could show me that plan in person, I pulled out my cash flow spreadsheet written neatly in black ink. I showed him how much we had coming in each month, how much we owed the IRS, and how much we owed our vendors. Instead of $5,000 a month, I proposed $75 the first month with a gradual increase each month. It would take a few years to pay it off.

This process of creating goals each month for how much we wanted to sell and how much we had to pay the IRS and our vendors was a game changer. In retrospect, I'm glad I had to learn this, even if it was the hard way.

I then slid my marketing grid across the table so he could see my commitment to turning this around. It was one page and clearly explained our yearly marketing plan. That is how simple the Reputation Matrix is.

I also showed him the newspaper article about our family-owned business, and he offered his first smile of the visit.

Looking back at my spreadsheet, Mr. Washington took off his black-framed glasses, folded his arms, and said, "You have done your homework, and I am going to accept your payment plan. However, if you miss one payment, we will be closing you down."

As he got up to leave, I put my finger up and said, "Wait right here; I have something for you." I ran to the back, grabbed a handful of chocolate candy kisses wrapped in pink cellophane and tied with a pink ribbon that had my business card attached. It was a marketing idea I learned from the trade publications: go beyond what people expect. Be exceptional. Mr. E. Washington offered another big smile.

The next hurdle was reaching out to each vendor to whom we owed money.

One company had sold us a high-tech copier that we could no longer afford. When I asked if they would take it back, they demanded full payment plus penalties for returning it early. I was forced to explain we were trying to avoid bankruptcy, and if they picked up the equipment by the first of the month, we would be able to get a small sum of money to them. Otherwise, they might lose out entirely. They accepted.

I also approached Consumer Credit Counseling Service (CCCS) because I had heard that if my father was under the "protection of CCCS," a lot of the phone calls and threatening letters would end. CCCS could help negotiate the debt from a high monthly payment to a substantially lower amount.

Vendors knew that once CCCS took over, the situation was serious. By having CCCS help us with the majority of these accounts, we were able to decrease the amount of money flowing out to repay vendors, using it instead to operate the business.

I followed that strategic move by telling each of our vendors that in order to avoid bankruptcy, we had created a payback schedule for each of them. Most plans started with fifteen dollars a month and increased as our anticipated sales increased. They accepted the new terms but threatened unanimously to sue us if we missed a payment.

From there, I turned to our business community to seek advice.

It began with a man named Greg, a CPA and tax advisor for a larger company who worked near our building. He advised us to contract out our payroll because the IRS looks favorably on that.

Other ideas flowed in from elsewhere in the Alexandria business community.

One such tip was to do a mailing to potential clients. I realized we couldn't afford a mass mailing, but we could do it for a select twenty-five associations. I looked up the businesses and their addresses and phone numbers, just as I had planned on my marketing grid.

The twenty-five we selected were within a five-mile range. We called each of them, introduced ourselves as the "printers for associations" and made sure to let them know we were conveniently "right around the corner." Each time, I politely asked if we could send them more information about our business, including the great article the newspaper had written about us.

When we hung up, I lined up the eight postcards I had designed. We didn't have the credit to buy new paper, so I found leftover paper, ran the postcards through the laser printer, and carefully cut them down to postcard size.

Each postcard contained our name, Carriage Trade Printing; our tagline, "Printers for Associations"; and our address and phone number. We mailed out the eight messages every Monday, Wednesday, and Friday:

1. The handwritten "We are neighbors! Great talking with you!"
2. "We deliver your printing for free."
3. "We store your printing for free."
4. "Celebrating thirty years in business."
5. "Your neighborhood printer for letterhead, envelopes, and business cards for associations."
6. "Sign up for our newsletter, 'Tips on Designing.'"
7. "We will call you to set up a time to show you our printing samples. We would love to earn your business."
8. The handwritten "I look forward to meeting with you soon." I sent this final mailing in a large envelope that contained a reprint of the article published the month before.

By the time I called to set up an appointment, each business had received all eight postcards. I arrived at each appointment dressed in black slacks and a white collared shirt. My sleeves were rolled up, my hair pulled back in a bun, and my glasses perched on my nose. This was to become my signature business look.

With me, I had a stack of printing samples, a hard copy of that newspaper article, and my three candy kisses with a business card attached. My question was always the same and I asked it with a smile: "What do we need to do to earn your business? We want to do business with you." All of them requested a quote to print a letterhead and envelopes, which we delivered the next day.

Slowly but surely, our plan was working.

Earlier, on my birthday, my father had given me a book, *The E-Myth*, by Michael Gerber. The subtitle was *Why Most Small Businesses Don't Work and What to Do About It.*

It became a cornerstone for us, instructing us on how to set up processes within the business. How does the job come in? How does it flow through the company? How do you deliver it to the client? All the processes needed to be recorded. By setting up these procedures, we didn't have to reinvent the wheel each time a new job came in. The business became more consistent in workflow and product delivery.

We spent the next few months recording the flow of work and the marketing process.

In so many ways I am almost grateful that we had to learn these lessons the hard way. It forced us to understand accounting, marketing, and the process of operating the print shop from the ground up. No longer did we wait for the one time a year that an accountant would reveal our profit and loss statements. I looked at them daily.

I ingested books, magazines, and tips from business colleagues as we started to turn the business around.

This experience was the best business education I ever received, but also the hardest.

Those times of testing taught us things we needed to know for the survival and future of my father's business. Among them were valuable marketing lessons that we used as we turned our company around and that I would use over and over again in my future business.

When my husband returned from the Gulf War, we managed to get stationed at Fort Belvoir, Virginia, for three years, which was in the same neighborhood as my father's company.

Then, in 1993, in the same month that we sent the final payment of back payroll taxes to Mr. E. Washington and the IRS, the US Army sent us to Savannah, Georgia.

All of our hard efforts had paid off, and we could move on with peace of mind. We did turn my father's company around. We avoided bankruptcy; we paid off all of the vendors and all of our back taxes. It took about three years, but we did it.

I'm grateful for the business lessons I learned in helping to save my father's company because they gave me the confidence to start my own company in Savannah dedicated to helping small business owners set and achieve their marketing goals.

I decided to open a public relations company because I saw how powerful that was for our family's business. I share those lessons learned with other small business owners to help them build positive word of mouth in the community and on-line, and to increase their sales, using my Reputation Matrix.

In June 2006, I was honored at the Savannah Area Chamber of Commerce as Entrepreneur of the Year. The Hospice Savannah nurse made arrangements to have my father in the audience. From the stage, I dedicated the award to him—to David Deshler Watson, Sr.

He died a month later.

CHAPTER 3

Meet the Reputation Matrix

There are countless ways to market your company. Most small business owners create a marketing plan that only consists of paid advertising and social media, and then they hope for word of mouth. What they don't realize is that there is another method of marketing called public relations, a.k.a. PR. With a PR strategy, positive word of mouth is the outcome, which means more new business referrals.

To build your yearly PR plan, you will need to leverage your good business news to create megapositive word of mouth.

Small business owners are usually very involved in their communities. They want to make sure it is a great place to live and work so they can attract employees. They want to make sure the schools are great places for their children.

One thing they often do is donate to a cause that will help make their community a better place.

Another is to hire new people.

Both are examples of notable actions that can be leveraged to create articles in your community paper.

Getting an article in the newspaper means that thousands of readers and online subscribers can get to know you and your company. Moreover, once the article is posted online, you can share it with your social media following to make the audience even greater. You now have gone from having a handful of people read about your news to having thousands learn about your good news, which will create positive buzz.

Your good news is now a conversation starter that leads to positive word of mouth in the community. Your potential customers will be talking to other potential customers about the great things they have heard about your company.

For decades I have helped small business owners enhance their reputation by deploying five proprietary strategies I call the Top Five Credibility Markers, a name I chose because they are all topics local media outlets tend to report on.

The Top Five Credibility Markers are as follows:

Awards. When you win an award, it shows that you are the best.

Authority. Giving educational talks and arranging speaking engagements show you are the expert in your industry.

Charity. When you partner with a local nonprofit, it shows you care about the community.

Hard news. Hard news highlights business milestones, such as hiring a new person or celebrating a business anniversary. These milestones show you are a growing, trusted company in the community.

Leadership. By participating in leadership programs or being involved with a local nonprofit organization on a board level, you show that you are reliable and should be trusted to be an appointed leader.

To start this yearly PR plan, create a list of all the great things that you are or could be doing in the community. Here is a checklist of questions:

- ✔ What awards can you win?
- ✔ Are you hiring anybody this year?
- ✔ Will your company make a charitable donation this year?
- ✔ Do you have a signature event?
- ✔ Do you or could you have an upcoming speech or workshop?
- ✔ Are you the president of a local nonprofit organization?
- ✔ Is your company celebrating its fifth, tenth, twentieth, twenty-fifth, or fiftieth anniversary this year?
- ✔ If you are a new business, will you have a grand opening?

These are all topics that the media often highlights.

You can place this information in the Reputation Matrix, which will serve as your yearly PR plan.

Here is how to create it:

The matrix should have January through December across the top. Down the left-hand side, list the Top Five Credibility Markers. The goal is to name one piece of news each month for a total of twelve media releases a year.

It can't be the same type of news each month.

Just like a balanced money portfolio of stocks, bonds, mutual funds, and investments, your PR plan must be balanced too. Don't plan on donating to a charity twelve times a year and expect coverage each month. The media might run the first release, but it's doubtful they will run it again and again.

Perhaps in January, your goal is to give a speech. Credibility marker: authority.

Perhaps in February, your goal is to apply for an award. Credibility marker: award.

Perhaps in March, your goal is to donate $1,000 to a charity. Credibility marker: charity.

Once you have a plan, you have to do the work on the front end: arrange that speech, apply for the award ahead of time, budget for that donation. The next step is to contact the media to let them know about your good news.

If the media considers this newsworthy content, they may decide to publish the information you gave them as an article, a news brief, or a column at no cost to you or your business. The hard truth is that sometimes the media only uses part of what you send, and sometimes they don't run it at all. However, if they do use the content, thousands will see it.

This is where PR differs from advertising. Ads are generated and paid for by a business. The business will know what day the ad will run and in what section. Ads secure guaranteed placement. Businesses often buy ads when they have an event or a big sale going on.

There is an old saying in the PR world: "You pay for advertising; you pray for PR."

The best way to build positive word of mouth is one of the best-kept secrets in the business world. Getting your name out is a necessity. When potential clients read about you in a positive light, it creates instant credibility that cannot be bought using advertising.

These Top Five Credibility Markers will get your good news and brand to come up in the search engines. This is one of the ways potential clients will research you and assess whether or not to do business with you, depending on what they find.

When people are looking for a product or service, they typically take the following steps:

1. Ask a friend.
2. Do online research.
3. Make a selection.

You want to be the company they select. Internet search results are a reflection of your reputation. And it's the organic search results that are important, not the paid ads.

Those results show up mostly by getting your good news into traditional media, which then ends up online. All these organic, nonpaid results build confidence on the part of the potential client.

This method will help bring up those organic hits with powerful reputation-building content that shows you are the authority in your field, you support charitable organizations, you are a leader, and your company is award winning and growing.

The more positive content that ends up online, the better chance it will show up when potential clients are researching you and your brand.

The power of your positive reputation is as imperative today as it was a hundred years ago. People still rely on word of mouth to make decisions on whether or not to buy from you.

This is the beginning of building your community and online presence.

CHAPTER 4

PR Pop Quiz: Twelve Assessment Questions

It's time for a PR pop quiz. The twelve simple questions below can help you assess how visible your business is in the community and online at this moment.

PR Assessment

Answer Yes or No

1. Does your community know about your company?
2. Does your good news show up when you do a Google search?
3. Do you have a repeatable tagline of ten words or fewer?
4. Do you have an organized group of businesses that you can rely on for referrals?
5. Do you know your keywords?

6. Do you post testimonials?
7. Do you have a strategic, yearly word-of-mouth plan?
8. Are you positioned as an authority in your field?
9. Are you active in leadership roles within the community?
10. Do you give back to the community?
11. Has your company won an award?
12. Do you let the local media know your positive business news?

If you answered *yes* to all of these questions, you are likely already experiencing positive word of mouth in the community and online. You get an A-plus.

Your company will benefit from this guidebook if the majority of answers are *no*.

CHAPTER 5

Start with a
Good Foundation

There are four main ways to build a good foundation.

Identify Branded Keywords

How well do you know your online reputation? The first step is to do an online search using your name and the name of your business. This is called a branded keyword search.

For example, my branded keyword search would be "Marjorie Young, Carriage Trade Public Relations Inc."

If you make an effort to use these branded keywords when building your reputation, potential clients are likely to hear and use these terms when they search for you online.

To put this in perspective, you'll need to use your branded keywords in all published content, including media releases, photo names/captions, videos, podcasts, and website copy. This is how potential clients will find positive information about you.

You should also do an unbranded keyword search of your products or services. My unbranded keyword search would be "Public Relations Savannah." During this search, all your local competition will also show up.

What are your results? Do your website and social media sites show up first? Are there any articles about your company on the first page? Are there pages and pages of unrelated search engine results?

Savvy potential customers who are searching your branded keywords know the difference between a paid advertisement and organic results. They understand that your business website is essentially a paid advertisement, highlighting the benefits and services you provide. The really powerful credibility builders will be articles, radio or TV interviews, and social media reviews of your business.

Google allows ten organic search results, and your goal is to fill those hits with positive articles about your company using the credibility markers. Your website and your profile on LinkedIn should also come up on the first page.

You want content to appear that shows the following:

Your company is award-winning.

Your company is growing.

You are a leader in the community.

You are considered an expert in your field.

You care about the community with your local charity involvement.

These all make positive, reputation-building content.

If you find all Top Five Credibility Markers on the first page, you get another A-plus. More likely, though, this is something most small business owners will have to work for.

Create Your Repeatable Tagline

This is the first step to creating positive word of mouth in the community and online. Consistency is key. If each team member says different things, the message to the community will be confusing. It's important that every employee says the same thing about what the company does.

Small business owners often have a hard time getting traction for their word-of-mouth referrals because they can't state in ten words or less what their company does. If you can't say it easily to the person in the mirror, how do you expect others to be able to talk about it?

As you saw with my father's company, we had to create a repeatable tagline before we saw marketing success. "Printers for Associations" demonstrated to associations that we specialized in their area of printing. This was also easily repeatable.

Knowing from experience that word of mouth is the number one way most small business owners get referrals, I highly recommend you spend some time developing your repeatable tagline.

Try this exercise. Have each person on your team write down on a piece of paper what your business does. Then read them all aloud. Are they all the same, or are there different messages?

When you're crafting your tagline, keep these five components in mind:

1. Make sure it doesn't sound like an ad. People trust something from the heart.
2. Make sure it fits in normal conversation.
3. Make sure it contains essential keywords that prospective clients will use to research you online.
4. Make sure it is memorable and repeatable, which will make it easier for people in the community to express it as you want it to be said.
5. Make sure it is a sentence of ten words or less.

One way to test your new repeatable tagline is to play the old-fashioned children's game of Telephone. Gather at least five people, and start by writing down your proposed tagline. Whisper it to one person, and then have that person whisper what they heard to the next person and so on. What the fourth or fifth person says is a good indication of what will be repeated in the community.

Is it what you whispered to the first person? If not, go back to the drawing board.

The repeatable tagline is the foundation for your other work.

Set Up a Laser-Focused Referral Group

A laser-focused referral group is a small group of specifically selected business owners that meets on a regular basis to share leads so the owners can spread the positive buzz about each other's company. Everybody in the group has the same type of clientele, and nobody in the group is in competition with the others.

For instance, if you own an audiovisual company that installs big-screen TVs in high-end homes, you might choose an indoor lighting company, a lawn service, a hardwood flooring company, and an interior painting company. All four of these companies should have one thing in common: they service high-end homeowners.

Often when one business is working on a job, a homeowner will ask for other recommendations pertaining to the home.

"Who would you recommend to paint my living room?" "Do you know of any great lawn services?" You can then refer the members of your referral group to the homeowner.

Strategically selecting a laser-focused referral group will increase your chances of a referral by the number of business owners in your group.

This kind of group is small but mighty. It is also free, unlike paid commercial networking groups.

This is one of the most underutilized marketing tools that the small business owner has available to him or her. I learned about this idea from Diana Morrison and Valerie Edgemon, community business owners who helped me set up my own group years ago.

By setting up a laser-focused referral group, you will learn about complementary businesses, and they will learn about yours. Over time, trust is built and referrals flow. You will be their eyes, ears, and advocates in the community, and they yours.

Setting up a no-fee referral group has five basic steps:

1. Make the decision to form a laser-focused referral group for the sole purpose of getting to know other business owners who share similar clientele in order to increase referrals.
2. Identify exactly what type of client the group will cater to. Is it a business owner (business-business)? Is it

a customer (business-consumer)? Is the client local? What gender is the client? What age? Is the client high-end? What is his or her education level? List as many traits as possible to clearly define the shared client.

3. Choose four business owners who are not in competition with anyone else in the proposed group. Make sure that each caters to the type of client you identified, that each is experienced, and that each has a good reputation. Try to select owners who are influencers in the community.

4. Reach out to the owners. Let them know you are often asked for referrals and would like the opportunity to meet with them to learn more about their company, and to tell them more about yours. After you meet with all four people separately, suggest a one-hour coffee or lunch meeting to introduce them to each other. When your group meets and you feel confident about refer-ring each other, suggest that you get together on a monthly or quarterly basis, making your laser-focused referral group official.

5. Create a yearly calendar for your meetings. You may decide to meet monthly at noon at a local coffee shop. On your agenda should be sharing the good news hap-pening in each company, sharing any new prospective clients in the community, and reporting on any referrals the members have recently made.

Collect Testimonials

Testimonials are positive reviews about you and your busi-ness that can be shared with and viewed online by potential clients.

They are basically the documented word of mouth of happy clients.

An easy place to begin is with current clients. Ask at least three to post a positive review on LinkedIn, Yelp, or Google. From there you can pull testimonials to your website and other social media outlets.

Third-party endorsements from clients are huge credibility builders.

A constant flow of new and positive testimonials on Google, Yelp, and other online sites will also help with your search engine rankings, meaning more relevant results on the first page.

Ideally, you will secure these testimonials before you kick off your yearly word-of-mouth PR campaign.

PART II:

The Power of the Reputation Matrix

CHAPTER 6

Create Your Yearly Word-of-Mouth PR Strategy

With your branded keywords, repeatable tagline, laser-focused referral group, and testimonials in place, you are ready to build your yearly word-of-mouth PR campaign. To do this we will use the Reputation Matrix.

If a yearly word-of-mouth PR plan sounds complicated, rest assured it isn't. Remember, the plan is just a one-page spreadsheet—the Reputation Matrix. Growing up in a small family-owned business, I know how busy owners are, but this one-page plan makes it very easy to follow through. I have successfully used this method with hundreds of small business owners over the past twenty-five years.

The goal here is to help you uncover your good news in each of these areas and place it on the PR plan.

Below is the template.

This will be the beginning of your yearly plan. The goal is to have one media release distributed each month, a total of twelve per year.

For example, you announce your new vice president in January. That would be listed in the Hard News row of the January column.

For February, you announce a $500 donation to a nonprofit. That would be listed in the Charity row, February column.

You don't have to have a communications degree to write a media release. If you have no idea where to begin, I have tips for you in chapter 12.

Year	Jan	Feb	Mar	Apr	May	Jun	Jul	Aug	Sept	Oct	Nov	Dec
Authority												
Awards												
Charity		ex: $500										
Hard News	ex: VP											
Leader												

Once the Reputation Matrix is filled out, you can easily see which media release needs to be sent each month and what you need to prepare for the next month.

Building your Reputation Matrix is crucial to creating a strategic flow of positive news for the local media throughout the year.

It is important to have this yearly word-of-mouth PR plan before you start submitting news releases to the local media. This is your cornerstone, and it needs to highlight your reputation by balancing out the Top Five Credibility Markers throughout the year.

Now, let's examine the five strategies you need for your Reputation Matrix.

CHAPTER 7

Credibility Marker: Authority

Strategy #1

The first strategy is to establish yourself as an authority. Here are some proven ideas.

You Are the Expert

Positioning yourself as an expert in your field is one of the most powerful word-of-mouth marketing strategies available to the small business owner.

You can accomplish this through educational marketing. This is not perceived as a direct effort to sell your products or services, but rather a way to enlighten your audience on valuable, need-to-know information that will help them in their business or personal lives.

By getting in front of your audience as an authority in your field, you do end up increasing your chances of making a sale.

They will see you as the subject matter expert and seek further advice as a paid client, trust you as a vendor, or tell others about the great information you presented to the group.

There are many opportunities to position yourself as an authority in your field. The top three are speaking in front of an audience, writing educational columns for the local paper, and writing a book.

For the typical small business owner, writing a book requires significantly more time, but the substantial positive word-of-mouth and media coverage will be worth it.

How to Be the Authority in Your Field

First, decide what educational tips will help people in their business or personal lives.

For example, if you are an accountant, you could give a speech to the local chamber of commerce on "Ten New Tax Laws Every Small Business Owner Must Know for the Upcoming Year."   You may have to reach out and arrange the speech yourself, but it is well worth the effort. If they select you to speak on their stage, it suggests they consider you an expert in your field. This will help build your credibility.

Often small business owners have a hard time constructing a speech. One simple way is to have a title such as "Ten Things to Know about (topic)." With a title like this, the audience expects to quickly learn valuable information that can help their business. They also know the speaker has a distinct beginning and ending. Top Ten list articles also are clicked on more often than others when posted online.

Many people are nervous about public speaking, at least initially. If you can overcome that fear, your positive reputation will soar.

Once you are selected to speak, send the host a typed, half-page bio in a sixteen-point readable font, large enough for somebody to easily read as they introduce you. This bio needs to be carefully thought out. It should include information about your business, how long you have been in business, where you went to school, and any awards or additional training you have received. This introduction will establish credibility and is the only time your business can be mentioned during the presentation.

You should also include some personal information in your bio, what PR folks call "touch points" that make you relatable.

Take this opportunity to state your business values. People want to do business with companies that share their values. For example, if your company has recently installed solar panels and you are speaking to a "green" organization, include that information in your short bio.

Once you are confirmed to speak and have sent in your bio, submit a press release to the newspaper announcing that you will be the featured speaker next month. Include your professional headshot. Hopefully the paper will include it in its calendar of business events.

Next, call the local TV station to see if they can bring you on to speak about the upcoming educational speech. Local stations usually have more than one spot for guests. You can invite a representative from the organization to which you are speaking to join you. Make sure to 1) share one or two tips from your speech during the short TV interview and 2) direct people to your website for more information.

An essential rule of thumb for speaking opportunities is that there must be no hint of an endorsement of your business. It must be 100 percent educational. If your talk is perceived as a sales pitch, you will lose credibility and will not be invited back.

If the host organization allows it, have a member of your team livestream your speech from one of your company's social media sites. This will show your authority among your followers, and if you tag the hosting organization, their followers can learn about you as well.

Get someone to take a photo of you speaking, so when you turn your speech into a column for the local newspaper afterward—which you should absolutely do—you have a great photo to accompany it. A picture of you at the podium shows power and authority. It also makes for a good social media post along with the ten tips you offered, even if you have also livestreamed your speech.

Capture your speech with a smartphone or a video camera. Then upload it to YouTube, and make sure to tag the speech with your name, your company's name, your services, your re-peatable tagline, and the title of the talk. These hits will show up when somebody is researching your brand.

The video file also can be emailed to the local cable company using an online file-sharing platform. Local cable TV is always looking for 100 percent educational content to run for free on its local cable channel.

Success Stories: Small Business Owners Positioning Themselves as the Authority

Here are some success stories to help you plan your path to becoming an authority in your community:

Host a Lecture Series. We were working with a retirement center that needed to figure out a way to present the facility to seniors on a casual basis. We developed a monthly lecture series that featured discussions led by residents and nonresi-dents about historical events that touched their lives. Topics ranged from World War II to exploring Antarctica. The magic of this campaign was that it allowed us to invite seniors and their adult children into the facility, where they were served a nice meal in an attractive dining room while listening to the speakers. We filmed the lectures and uploaded them online. The local newspaper often did features on the sessions, gain-ing the center even more visibility. For its part, the retirement home was able to collect names and make direct sales calls afterward.

Present Livestream Educational Seminars. When Facebook Livestream first appeared on the scene, we jumped on the opportunity to line up a client in the technology industry for a talk to the local SCORE chapter (a group of volunteers that mentor small business owners) on "The Top Ten Ways to Avoid Being Hacked," using this new feature. We had a small in-house audience, but by going live with Facebook, we reached a much larger audience that interacted and asked questions via the comment section. This tactic allowed the technology company to show how progressive it was as the first local firm to livestream a lecture.

Write a Book. When the green movement was starting to emerge, a few construction companies adopted new technology to reduce their carbon footprint. The public was skeptical and unaware of the long-term benefits of going green. As part of the effort to educate people on the importance of these developments, the CEO of one local company wrote a book. The CEO was invited to do a television interview as a local green champion, and numerous media outlets wrote articles about the grand opening of the company's next green construction project.

Write a Column. Our company encouraged the executive director of a local shelter for teen runaways to write an opinion piece for the local newspaper every November during National Runaway Prevention Month discussing the number of homeless teens in our city. She emphasized the economic implications for the city due to crime. This column continues to aid the shelter's fundraising efforts and creates significant buzz in the philanthropic community.

Create a TV Show. When I was helping turn my father's company around, I reached out to numerous small business owners in the community and asked for their advice on payroll, marketing, purchasing, credit, and how to run a company. These busy owners took time to share their best practices with me. When I decided to start my own company, I also decided to create a TV show that would highlight this powerful information. During the show, I interviewed small business owners on camera, and they shared their best tips and advice for growing a company. I, in turn, suggested ways they could market their companies using these word-of-mouth strategies. Today, twenty-five years later, we still host our monthly show, *Open For Business*, only now it is 100 percent online. This exposure helps position us as the authority, and it creates positive word of mouth within the small business community.

Authority and the Reputation Matrix

To bring this back to your Reputation Matrix, plan it out so you commit to two speeches and two mirroring columns each year. This amounts to four yearly credibility hits in the community and online.

If you are an accountant, for example, you could have one speech in January on "New Tax Regulations" and another in July on "Five Overlooked Small Business Deductions."

Your column on "New Tax Regulations" could run in April and the "Five Overlooked Small Business Deductions" in October.

Your matrix will start to take shape.

REPUTATION MATRIX 2020©

Year	Jan	Feb	Mar	Apr	May	Jun	Jul	Aug	Sep	Oct	Nov	Dec
Authority	Speech			Column			Speech			Column		
Awards												
Charity												
Hard News												
Leader												

CHAPTER 8

Credibility Marker: Awards

Strategy #2

The next strategy is to win awards. Here are some proven ideas.

Award-Winning Company

Awards are something you earn if a local, state, or national organization considers you to be the best in your field.

Winning an award is a huge third-party endorsement, and the organization that gives out the award will usually submit a media release and post the information online to publicize the news. Those posts and any posts generated by media coverage will be shared and reshared. Thus, the positive word of mouth spreads.

Awards are a key way to build credibility and highlight your reputation.

How to Win an Award

There are several organizations that might grant you an award, such as your local chamber of commerce, your trade association, local nonprofits, or local media, to name a few.

Take the time to research all the potential awards you can win. Start by calling or researching your local chamber and your industry trade associations to find out about award categories and timelines.

Award applications are often lengthy and time-consuming, but if you win, it will all be rewarded with significant positive press and word of mouth in the community and online.

Over the past twenty-five years, I have been involved in judging numerous local award nominations. One thing that always surprises me is how few businesses apply for these community awards. That means if you submit a nomination, you might have a good chance of winning. Nothing ventured, nothing gained.

Your local chamber of commerce likely has a yearly awards competition, such as "Small Business of the Year," "Entrepreneur of the Year," or "New and Emerging Business of the Year," for which you can nominate your company.

Also, almost every industry has a trade association that offers annual awards. You can be nominated or nominate yourself. If you win, the association will publicize it, and it will end up online, which helps your reputation both within your industry and among potential clients.

Your company can also create its own awards to bestow on others. Maybe you give a $1,000 scholarship to a local high school senior. This is good news that you can create, and it will most likely be picked up by the local media and shared on social media.

Many communities also have a city magazine. Often these magazines have a yearly contest along the lines of "Best of" awards. The businesses and/or professionals that receive the most votes from the community are named "Best of" in their categories. It's one more way for a small business owner to get positive word of mouth.

If you do win an award and the organization submits the good news to the local media, your business should also send out a media release announcing the award. Include your branded keywords in the headline so there is a better chance of your information appearing at the top of the search engine results when potential clients research your company.

When the article(s) about the award runs, make sure to post it on your website, share it on social media outlets, and make copies to use on your sales calls.

You also can include information about awards you have won on your email signature and your business cards.

If you have a physical office, have the article framed and placed in the waiting area or conference room. You will be amazed by the number of people who comment on it.

Success Stories: Winning Awards

Here are some examples of award success stories:

Family-Owned Business Award. We worked with a family-owned veterinary practice that was celebrating one hundred years in business. In addition to the positive press about turning one hundred and the stories that went with it, we found a family business association that gave awards every year. The veterinary practice applied and was recognized nationally as the best century-long, family-owned business. National and local media ran several stories about it. Plus, winning a national award generated a huge amount of positive word of mouth.

40 Under 40 Award. Many communities have an award sponsored by their newspaper called "40 Under 40." This award is presented to forty young professionals each year. The application is lengthy, but it's worth the time to fill it out. The winners receive extensive publicity. Our employee was selected locally. A year later she was selected on a state level as a "40 Under 40" up-and-coming leader. Awards build visibility and huge credibility.

$1,000 Grant. A few years ago, our firm was asked to help develop a campaign for a large convenience store chain. This company saw the healthy nutritional trend moving across America and made the shift to carry and market healthy snacks in their stores. To get that message out, we partnered with a local nonprofit dedicated to reducing obesity in the city and decided to create an educational series on health. With each lecture, the convenience store also awarded a $1,000 grant to a local nonprofit dedicated to improving health through exercise and nutrition. The media ran a story to let the community know about each upcoming lecture; it also ran a story about each $1,000 grant.

Proclamation. A proclamation is a great way to raise visibility about a cause or an important event. We employed this tactic for a nonprofit organization that was celebrating thirty years in service. We contacted city hall to get a proclamation issued.

Then the mayor read it during the organization's thirtieth anniversary celebration before a roomful of guests and the media.

Chamber Award. One of the most memorable awards I have won was in July 2006. The chamber informed me that I was named Entrepreneur of the Year. Earlier that year, my father had been diagnosed with stage 4 lung cancer and came to live with me under hospice care. On the night of my award, the hospice nurse suggested that she bring him to the ceremony in a wheelchair. He made it, and somehow I climbed to the podium and dedicated the award to my father, without crying, in front of a few hundred people. I now have a forever photo of my father and me on the front page of the paper.

Awards and the Reputation Matrix

Start by researching when the awards will be announced and when applications are due. Place these dates on the Reputation Matrix. I would recommend applying for two awards a year: one locally, the other through your trade association.

If you win one or both, issue a media release during the month it will be announced.

REPUTATION MATRIX 2020©

Year	Jan	Feb	Mar	Apr	May	Jun	Jul	Aug	Sep	Oct	Nov	Dec
Authority	Speech			Column			Speech			Column		
Awards		Chamber										Trade Association
Charity												
Hard News												
Leader												

CHAPTER 9
Credibility Marker: Charity

Strategy #3

A third strategy is to get involved with charities. Here are some proven ideas.

How to Get Involved with a Charity

Within every community there are numerous charity, or non-profit, organizations. These charities help to enhance the lives of people and animals in the area.

If you're not already working with a charity, find one that aligns with your values and get involved. Let the media know about the partnership and how your company is helping to support this charity by donating time or money. Make the story about the nonprofit, and the media will often jump on the chance to cover a feel-good story.

When potential clients read about your outreach to local charities, they see that you care about your community.

For every business my team advises, it is almost a requirement that they strategically align with a nonprofit. Because many of the CEOs don't feel comfortable submitting a media release about donating money to a charity, I often have to remind them how beneficial this type of coverage is for gaining local recognition for the charity as well.

Success Stories: Charity

Here are some success stories to help you plan your involvement with charities:

Cooking for Charity. One of my favorite charitable campaigns was a monthly cooking class held by a chef who owned a local restaurant. Tickets to the monthly classes were $100 each, but this included a full-course meal and a private lesson on preparing it. The chef invited a different nonprofit each month and donated 100 percent of that night's profits to them. Media filmed the demonstrations and interviewed the nonprofit organization about the great opportunity to raise money. This effort earned the chef and the restaurant great buzz in the community.

Signature Event for a Nonprofit. Another possibility is to begin a signature event for which you assume the role of title sponsor. This takes a huge amount of legwork, but the positive word of mouth it builds is incredible. To give you an idea of how quickly it can grow, a local 5K walk/run sponsored by one local business, started with a few hundred people and now attracts runners and walkers by the thousands. None of these participants can miss the name of the company—it's in the name of the race.

Celebrity Involvement. If you are reading this as a leader with a nonprofit and you are lucky enough to get a celebrity to participate in your local fundraising event, it elevates visibility not only for your nonprofit, but also for the city. Each year a group that advocates for folks with different abilities hosts a one-mile walk around the park. The group was able to use a personal connection to get a huge television personality to be the grand marshal of the walk.

People who had been previously unaware of the local charity came out to see the celebrity and learned a great deal about the organization through the experience.

Employees Volunteer. A local company reached out to a local nonprofit and donated their employees to help with the organization's facility. Sometimes the employees help paint the building; sometimes they help fix a fence. They usually spend all day there, and the media loves to cover these happy stories. The word of mouth gets started in the media and continues with the employees and the folks at the nonprofit organization.

Car Show Raises Money. A group of car enthusiasts selected a local private school to host a car show on its grounds.

The group arrived with their beautiful automobiles, and hundreds of people visited the campus to see the cars. They also got to see how beautiful the school is. TV stations and local newspapers covered the event, and it generated significant buzz on social media.

Charity and the Reputation Matrix

Review the list of charities you help. Which ones do you donate to every year? Which ones do you help with a service day?

It is recommended that you have two charity media releases each year, preferably spread at least four months apart.

Fill in the blocks when you plan to donate or dedicate a service day. Generating a happy story for the local media can be as simple as a check presentation.

REPUTATION MATRIX 2020©

Year	Jan	Feb	Mar	Apr	May	Jun	Jul	Aug	Sep	Oct	Nov	Dec
Authority	Speech			Column			Speech			Column		
Awards		Chamber										Trade Association
Charity			$1000 Donation								Service Day	
Hard News												
Leader												

CHAPTER 10

Credibility Marker: Hard News

Strategy #4

A fourth strategy is to highlight your hard news. Here are some proven ideas.

What Is Hard News?

The next part of creating your yearly plan is deciding what hard news you might generate throughout the year.

In the media world, hard news means news generated from the business side of your company. The business section of your community newspaper often runs information about new businesses, ribbon cuttings, new employees, promotions, anniversaries, new technology, new office or sales locations, and even new clients or contracts. Don't hesitate to let the media know by sending a media release to the business editors.

They are on the lookout for this type of news, and anything used in print will also be posted online.

Hard news is powerful reputation-building content. The media loves to use it.

Success Stories: Hard News

Here are some success stories to help you identify hard news so you can use it to build word of mouth:

Make an Announcement. A car dealership announced its expansion into the next city. It also announced its new product line of cars.

Observe a Milestone. When my company celebrated its twentieth anniversary, we invited nine other companies that were celebrating twenty years to a party. It was a great representation of the success of small businesses in Savannah overall, and we invited the mayor to give a toast.

Announce a Launch. A technology company announced the launch of its new website. The story ran both in the newspaper and online.

Announce a New Hire. A local marketing company announced its summer intern and received coverage in print and online.

Stage an Event. A local mall installed a new carousel for its food court. It staged a ribbon cutting, and three local TV stations came to cover it. This was viewed by thousands and created positive word of mouth for the mall.

Celebrate an Anniversary. When my father's company turned thirty years old, I wrote a media release and sent it to the business section of the community newspaper. It resulted in a reporter writing a long feature article with a photo that we used in future sales presentations. The paper's organic, third-party endorsement helped to turn my father's company around. It generated a huge amount of credibility and new clients.

Grand Opening. A metal recycling plant opened in the community, and the local newspaper ran the story on the front page. The photograph featured the governor of the state with the owners, and the article remarked on how many jobs the business was creating. If you have a new business that is about to open, create an event to recognize it. Invite the public. Invite the mayor to cut the ribbon. Or get really creative like the next example.

Ribbon Cutting. We conducted a ribbon cutting and a grand opening for a national retailer that specializes in the great outdoors. Our job was to get media to the event. By the time the day arrived, the public was so excited about this opening that people started lining up at 5:00 a.m. for a 9:00 a.m. opening. The local media went live with these early birds on their morning shows, which drew an even bigger crowd. There were 2,500 lined up to enter the store when it opened. To reward the anticipation, instead of a typical ribbon cutting, we had an ace bow-and-arrow archer split the ribbon in two.

Hard News and the Reputation Matrix

Look at your upcoming potential hard news items. If you know you will be promoting somebody to vice president of marketing, you can aim to announce that in May. If you know you will hire a new director of technology in March or April, add that to the Reputation Matrix to announce a few months later—maybe June. If your anniversary is in September, add it to the matrix. It is ideal to distribute at least three or four hard news releases throughout the year.

If more hard news happens in your company, don't hold back. Go ahead and submit that info to the media, but space it out as best as you can.

REPUTATION MATRIX 2020©

Year	Jan	Feb	Mar	Apr	May	Jun	Jul	Aug	Sep	Oct	Nov	Dec
Authority	Speech			Column			Speech			Column		
Awards		Chamber										Trade Association
Charity			$1000 Donation								Service Day	
Hard News					New Hire	New Hire			Anniversary			
Leader												

CHAPTER 11

Credibility Marker: Leadership

Strategy #5

The fifth strategy is to be a visible leader. Here are some proven ideas.

How to Be a Leader

Highlighting your leadership responsibilities outside of your business is another positive way to be seen in the community. Leadership roles can range from elected positions to appointments. If your company is not involved in any such roles, find somewhere that you or another member of your team can get plugged in.

Success Stories: Leadership

Here are some success stories to help you plan how to leverage your team's leadership roles into your Reputation Matrix:

Get Appointed to a Board. When a business owner is involved in a local nonprofit and gets appointed to the organization's board of directors as president or a contributing member, it creates a great opportunity to send out a media release. The nonprofit may send out a media release, but if it does not plan to, you can announce the news. When the community reads about your leadership, this will bolster your company's credibility and visibility.

Get Elected. When I started my business, the first thing I did was to join the local small business chamber, and I was eventually asked to become president. In this role, I was able to reach out to other small business chambers in the region and coordinate networking events. I selected the small business chamber because its membership included other business owners, which was my target audience. In addition to helping us get media coverage, it expanded my network to hundreds of people I might never have connected with otherwise.

Apply for Leadership Programs. Most cities have leadership programs, and it is worth the time it takes to apply. These yearly programs will connect you with other up-and-coming leaders in the community. The names of the selected leaders also end up in the local media and online.

Start Your Own. Maybe there is an organization that needs to be started to make your community a better place.

Leadership and the Reputation Matrix

If you are involved with an organization and have just achieved the level of a board position or an elected position, call and find out if the group plans to announce the new leadership or board of directors. If so, find out what month that media release will go out. If not, find out when the information can be made public and write your own. Either way, add it to the Reputation Matrix.

REPUTATION MATRIX 2020©

Year	Jan	Feb	Mar	Apr	May	Jun	Jul	Aug	Sep	Oct	Nov	Dec
Authority	Speech			Column			Speech			Column		
Awards		Chamber										Trade Association
Charity			$1000 Donation								Service Day	
Hard News					New Hire	New Hire			Anniversary			
Leader								Board of Directors				

Notice how easy it is to see what action items you need to accomplish each month when you follow this checklist:

- ✔ January—your goal is to give a speech.
- ✔ February—you will nominate your own business for a chamber award.
- ✔ March—your company will donate $1,000 to the charity you are involved with.
- ✔ April—your goal is to write and submit a column for the local paper.
- ✔ May—you will announce your company's newest hire.
- ✔ June—you will announce another recent hire.
- ✔ July—your goal is to give another speech.
- ✔ August—you will make sure that your board involvement with the nonprofit is announced.
- ✔ September—you will announce your business anniversary.
- ✔ October—your goal is to write another educational column for the local paper.
- ✔ November—your business team will have a nonprofit service day.
- ✔ December—you will nominate your company for a trade association award.

By trickling out one media release a month, you will start to increase your visibility in the community and online, which leads to positive word-of-mouth buzz for you.

Creating word of mouth is the first step. The next step is sustaining word of mouth, which is covered in Part III.

PART III:
Sustaining Word of Mouth

CHAPTER 12

Start Spreading the News

Now that you have created your annual word-of-mouth PR plan using all five Credibility Markers on this Reputation Matrix, you will need to implement it.

Post your one-page Reputation Matrix where you can see it to remind you to prepare for and submit one media release each month to the local media and influencers.

Also put your action items on your calendar or task list.

From here, it takes four steps to implement it and get the word out.

1. **Do Your Research.** Find the email address and telephone number of the business editor of your local newspaper and connect with that person. Let the editor know you realize he or she is busy, but say that you want to ensure you have the correct email address for media releases. Ask how big the photos should be. Usually for newspapers it is about one or two megabytes. Editors will appreciate you taking the time to verify this information. Research the on-line *influencers* who have a local fan base. Start following them on their social media platforms. These influencers usually have a very loyal following, and if you are able to get them to talk about your service or product, it will be a huge boost to your positive word of mouth and reputation.

2. **Write the Media Release**. Next, write your release. Since you are reporting on your company's good news, you will want to write it in the third person, just the way a reporter would write a news story. Reporters use Associated Press (AP) style when writing articles. If you learn AP style, your news will have a better chance of getting picked up in the local media.

Editors are looking for something that gets to the point and is fewer than four hundred words, which is about one page. They want to know what the news is straightaway. For example, the headline might be "Company Names Mary Smith VP of Marketing." They will then want to know more about Mary and her duties, what she did before she came to work for you, where she grew up, and a sentence about her family and hobbies. Be sure to include your contact information at the end of the press release in case they have questions or want to interview Mary.

The news release for a community media outlet should be written so the public can easily understand the information. The sentences should be short and to the point. Write for a sixth grade audience so folks can quickly process the message.

Stay focused. If you are announcing a new hire, just announce a new hire. Don't try to include your newly designed website. Stick to one item of news per release and spread other news out over the months.

If you are still feeling overwhelmed about what this should look like, I have included a sample press release at the end of the chapter. Here are a few more tips:

Ten Additional Tips for a Media Release
- Make sure your headline is newsworthy.
- Make sure to include your branded keywords in the headline.

- Don't use superlatives.
- Don't use exclamation marks.
- Don't use multiple colors or bold fonts. The media just wants the facts. They will decide how important it is. Your writing has to support this.
- Triple-check that all the spelling and verb tenses are correct.
- Include your boilerplate at the bottom of the press release. This is three to four sentences about your company—who owns it, when it was founded, your location, your website, and a phone number. The media usually will cut this contact information when the online article runs. Please know that this is standard practice for the media. If you call and complain that they didn't include everything in the article, they will suggest that you buy an ad. However, you should post the full version of your media release on your website so the search engines find it too.
- Make sure the text is aligned on the left. If you indent, the media will just have to undo your formatting. Make it easy for them.
- Include your website address. If media outlets use your release and post it online, a link will drive traffic to your website. Make sure to write out the URL, e.g., https://carriagetradepr.com/ and not carriagetradepr.com.
- A press release can also be written in bullet points to cover who, what, where, when, why, and how. Just make sure it's clear to the editor what the news is. The local newspaper receives hundreds of releases each day, and not all are picked up. You have to submit a well-written release to be considered for publication.

3. **Distribute the Media Release to Media Contacts and Influencers.** When your media release is 100 percent ready, create an email to your contact at the newspaper. Copy and paste the media release into the body of the email, and attach it as a Word document. Do not attach it as a PDF. A PDF cannot be copied and pasted quickly and may result in the release not being used. You want to make this as easy as possible for the news staff.

   In the subject line, write the name of the influencer or reporter for whom the release is intended and who it is from. Also include the headline of the media release.

   Double-check to make sure your content is 100 percent newsworthy, with no hint of endorsement.

   Use the body of your email to write a note to the editor about why the release is newsworthy. Then put the release below the note.

   Be sure to attach the desired photo in your email to the editor, keeping the file size under 2 megabytes if it is for a newspaper.

   Make sure to name the image with your branded words so the file name reads "Mary Smith, Company Name.jpg."

   If you have other community newspapers or media outlets you want to send it to, do not CC or even BCC your media list. Send one media release at a time to one specific reporter or influencer. You will have a better chance of getting your information published if you take the time to connect with a name.

If your first media outlet does not pick up the news release, find another outlet and pitch it to that one. If it doesn't get picked up at all, you can always post your content online.

There are numerous free sites that publicists and companies use to post media releases. Seeking these out will also help your chances of appearing on search engines.

You should also distribute your media release to relevant trade association publications. There is a good chance they will pick it up and post it online, which will also help build your online reputation. If you have a charitable event coming up, make sure you get the information to local magazines at least two months in advance. Local newspapers need less lead time.

You should also use the media release to send to local television morning shows. They tend to book up very quickly, so make sure to arrange those interviews well in advance.

4. **Post on Social Media.** Once your media release information runs in the local newspaper or on television, share it on all of your social media platforms. Include a link to your hard-earned, third-party endorsement. This is where the word of mouth will amplify immensely.

Sample Media Release
Carriage Trade Public Relations® Marks 25th Anniversary

(SAVANNAH, GA) Carriage Trade Public Relations® Inc. will observe its twenty-fifth anniversary on March 6, marking a quarter century of service to the region's small business community.

As a lead-up to the anniversary, Marjorie Young, president, will publish *Reputation Matrix*, a step-by-step guidebook to help small businesses increase their visibility, credibility, and positive word of mouth in the community and online. Once released, the book will be available on Amazon.

"I started my own company after helping turn my father's small business around. I saw the power of public relations and wanted to make it accessible to other business owners," said Young.

As a newly single young mother, Young was an early adopter of the virtual office and the power of search engines in spreading positive word of mouth online.

In addition to growing a company and pioneering the power of the internet, Young has been active in the community, having served as president of the Small Business Chamber, chair of the Small Business Council, and chair of Savannah SCORE. Other past and present board involvement includes Leadership Savannah, Hospice Savannah, Dawn's Daughter Leadership Academy, Small Business Development Center Advisory Board, and Rotary Club of Savannah.

She has also won numerous awards: Business Advocate of the Year and Entrepreneur of the Year from the Savannah Area Chamber of Commerce, Small Business of the Year and Savannah Community Star Award from the *Savannah Morning News*, and Buy Local Advocate of the Year from Buy Local Savannah.

She holds a certification in crisis communications from the Public Relations Society of America and hosts frequent PR boot camps and webinars to empower business owners and nonprofit organizations to take control of their reputation, brand, and message.

Young is a graduate of the University of Maryland with a degree in journalism and a minor in fine art. In her spare time, she enjoys hiking and painting, and in 2016 she hiked the Camino de Santiago in Spain, a 500-mile trek.

About Carriage Trade Public Relations®, Inc.

Carriage Trade Public Relations®, Inc., is Savannah's premier reputation management company founded in 1995 by Marjorie Young to help businesses increase their visibility, credibility, and positive word of mouth in their community and globally online through its proprietary Reputation Matrix method. For more information, contact https://carriagetradepr.com/; 912-844-9990.

EPILOGUE

Nothing Ventured, Nothing Gained

So there you have it, the word-of-mouth secrets that I have used for decades to help small business owners, large businesses, nonprofits, and publicly traded companies. It is a plan that creates positive word of mouth in the community and online. A plan that helped turn my father's company around. A plan that will make you a local celebrity.

The more positive things you do, the more positive talk and top-of-mind awareness it creates. Having positive articles written or published about you also helps when you make sales calls because your prospects have already heard good things about you and your company.

Remember to ask yourself if any of your good deeds could become "news" in the local media. You will be surprised how much news you were leaving on the table. Think like a reporter, and ask yourself, "Is this a story?" No matter how you get it there, all of it should end up online to boost your positive reputation. Let the world know.

This Reputation Matrix is the foundation of all other marketing. If you don't have a good reputation, it is very difficult to create sustainable sales.

As with anything great, it takes time.

The small business owner who commits to following the Reputation Matrix will wonder why he or she hasn't used these strategies before. These proven strategies create the word-of-mouth buzz that generates the majority of new business.

Congratulations on taking the next step in growing your company. Congratulations on taking a chance for positive change by reading this guidebook, *Reputation Matrix*.

Since incorporating in 1995, my favorite business saying has been "Nothing ventured, nothing gained." If you never do something new, I guarantee you will remain where you are.

Buckle up your seat belts; it's time to roll.

Acknowledgments

David Deshler Watson Sr.
Carol Stuart Watson
Carol Christine Young PhD
John Watson
David Watson Jr.
Jamie Stuart
Lynn Towle
Monty and Stacy Wilkinson
Nancy Fellenz
Gale Baldwin
Richard Braithwaite
Diana Morrison
Valerie Edgemon
Mary Miltiades
Terrass "Razz" Misher
Nipuna Ambanpola
Janet Ricciuti
Melissa Gratias, PhD

Roy Austin
Henry DeVries
Chris McMillian
Tom and Suzana Barton
Chris Helton
Michael Siegel
SCORE
University of Georgia Small Business Development Center
Lisa Sepe, CHPC
Anastasia R Kontos
Elaine Longwater

ABOUT THE AUTHOR

Marjorie Young

In 1995, Marjorie Young founded Carriage Trade Public Relations Inc., a PR firm that specializes in reputation marketing strategies.

In 2017, the Savannah Area Chamber of Commerce awarded her the Helen V. Head, Small Business Advocate of the Year. In 2013, the *Savannah Morning News* named Carriage Trade PR the Small Business of the Year. In 2006, Marjorie won Entrepreneur of the Year from the Savannah Area Chamber of Commerce. In 2011, *Savannah Morning News* named her Savannah's Community Star. She also was named a Georgia Woman Entrepreneur finalist by the University of Georgia, and one of the Top Ten Women in Savannah by AWWIN, Inc.

Marjorie is also the past president of the Small Business Chamber, chair of the Small Business Council, and past chair of Savannah SCORE. Other past and present board involvement includes Leadership Savannah, Hospice Savannah, Dawn's Daughter, and Rotary Club of Savannah.

She holds frequent PR boot camps and webinars, which empower business owners and nonprofit organizations to take control of their PR, brand, and message.

Marjorie has a certification in crisis communications from the Public Relations Society of America.

She is celebrating twenty-five years in business.

She graduated from the University of Maryland with a degree in journalism and a minor in fine art. In her spare time, Marjorie enjoys hiking and painting, and in 2016 she walked the Camino de Santiago in Spain, a five-hundred-mile trek.

CPSIA information can be obtained
at www.ICGtesting.com
Printed in the USA
LVHW022247060820
662367LV00017B/570